the Journey

the Journey

discovering emotional and spiritual health after disability

a workbook

Jenny Smith, M.Ed.
author of *Live the Impossible*

SIGNIFICANT
- PUBLICATIONS -

The Journey:
Discovering Emotional and Spiritual Health after Disability
By Jenny Smith
Published by Significant Publications
Copyright © 2024 by Jenny Smith. All rights reserved.

ISBN PRINT: 978-1-7370867-3-4
ISBN EPUB: 978-1-7370867-4-1
Library of Congress Control Number: 2023923116

No part of this publication may be reproduced, stored in a retrieval system or transmitted in any form or by any means, electronic, mechanical, photocopying, recording, scanning or otherwise, except as permitted under Section 107 or 108 of the 1976 United States Copyright Act, without the prior written permission of the publisher. For permission requests, contact Jenny@JennySmithRollsOn.com.

This workbook is not intended as a substitute for professional medical or mental health services. If expert assistance is needed, please seek out a qualified professional.

Cover and typesetting by Jenneth Dyck

Edited by Kathy Burge and Elizabeth Trotter

This book may be purchased in bulk for proper promotional, educational, or business use. Please email Jenny Smith at Jenny@JennySmithRollsOn.com for more information.

Table of Contents

Introduction 9
Why Take Time to Reflect? 13
    Activity: Timeline 16
Naming What We've Lost 21
Journey of Grief 27
    Activity: Lament (Optional)...37
Change and Transition 43
Paradox 51
Stress, Trauma, and Coping Strategies 57
Refill Your Cup 71
Finding Meaning and Purpose 75
Conclusion 81
Appendix 1: Additional Resources 85
Appendix 2: Suggested Schedule for Groups 87
Appendix 3: Group Introduction and Rules 89
References 91
About the Author 93

Note to Reader

This workbook uses the term disability to include a physical condition that alters one's lifestyle or interaction with their surrounding environment. This includes, but is not limited to, paralysis, vision or hearing loss, Parkinson's disease, chronic pain, multiple sclerosis, Crohn's or ulcerative colitis, muscular dystrophy, brain injury, arthritis, amputations, and neurological or autoimmune disorders. Some people never receive a diagnosis for the symptoms that significantly impact their life.

Introduction

For over a decade I worked with people who live and work overseas in a cross-cultural context. They must learn a new language and culture. They experience the loss of friends and family members and may lose connection to beloved traditions. They must learn a new system of government, healthcare, and transportation.

The known becomes unknown. Unnavigable.

Simply making it through one day can be a challenge—and a small victory. Everything takes more time. More work. More concentration. More energy.

I helped my able-bodied coworkers name these challenges and grieve their losses. But grieving isn't where the process ends. Ultimately, the goal is for people to thrive in their new surroundings. They must find new activities they enjoy and peers with whom they can relate. They make new friends, become fluent in the language, and learn to live without their favorite treats like chocolate chips or peanut butter. As they do so, they shift from the unfamiliar to the familiar.

One day, I was sitting in front of the computer attending a training about cultural adaptation. Suddenly, I was struck by the parallels between living cross-culturally and transitioning to life with a disability.

Who is helping people with disabilities transition to a new way of life?

I turned off the camera in the middle of the training. My heart hurt for the thousands of people who navigate the new world of disability without support.

My journey with disability began when I was sixteen years old after I sustained a C6-7 spinal cord injury that left me paralyzed from the chest down and without the use of my hands. I had entered the world of disability without training on how to survive.

Those of us with disabilities also must learn a new language, one full of medical terminology. Many people lose close relationships with friends and family. Traditions are lost. Each day can feel overwhelming. Life is difficult, requires more energy, and everything we do takes longer. It takes time to understand government assistance, healthcare, and transportation. We celebrate the smallest victories, but our favorite food may be just out of reach—literally.

Why hadn't I seen the parallels before?

The cross-cultural workers I supported had months of training and preparation before they moved. We intentionally scheduled time to talk about their emotional and spiritual health in their new location.

But a disability occurs without notice. We have no training or preparation to make this transition. We don't learn about loss or how to grieve. The physical overshadows the emotional.

This workbook will give you tools to cope with the emotional impact of a physical disability.

Let's take this journey together. We'll traverse the paths of emotional and spiritual health in this foreign land called Disability.

Why Take Time to Reflect?

I have great respect for the past. If you don't know where you've come from, you don't know where you're going.

— Maya Angelou —

After an unexpected disability or chronic physical condition, our journey may seem to take on a life of its own. Doctors give medical diagnoses that are unfamiliar and terrifying. Family—if you are fortunate enough to have a supportive family—is concerned for your (and their) future. Maybe you remember when the doctor stated matter-of-factly, "The chance of a full recovery is unlikely." Or a specialist said, "Your condition will only continue to decline."

Whatever the circumstances, a flurry of activity likely followed. Surgery. Diagnostic testing. Physical and occupational therapy. Your home may be inaccessible and unfamiliar. You experience many losses and few gains. The truth of this unexpected life becomes all too real. It is too heavy of a burden to carry alone.

While outbursts of anger, frustration, sadness, and despair might be present, the focus is on our physical body. Little time is offered—or available—to process what we experience internally.

Let's set aside some time to reflect upon this unexpected journey. Reflecting is an opportunity to process your thoughts and feelings. It's a chance to look back on events, relationships, and emotions with honesty and ask how the current circumstances have changed you. Because you *are* different. Your physical abilities may be different. Your identity, your job, and your relationships may have changed.

Remembering and reflecting upon the story of our journey can help us look back so we can move forward into this unexpected life. What can we take from our experience that will make us more resilient? Can we name what we have lost? Do we know what we are grieving? Or have we buried those feelings because there hasn't been time—or the desire—to process them?

You may not see it now, but this journey is worth the time and effort.

Personal Reflection Questions

- What do you hope to accomplish or receive from this time of reflection?

- What thoughts and emotions do you have when you think about this process?

- Is something holding you back from being honest with yourself, the group members, or people close to you about your journey?

Activity: Timeline

Before we can determine where we are going, we need to look back on where we've been. A timeline is one way to start the process of reflecting.

On a large piece of paper or poster board, create a timeline of the period of time you want to process. Use a computer or tablet with assistive devices, if necessary. If you need help completing the timeline, ask someone you trust to help you. You may begin with the onset of your disability or a time before that event.

> *Points to include:*
>
> - Significant events (personal, health, work, national and international events)
> - Relationship changes (friendships, family, dating, marriage, divorce, spiritual condition)
> - Physical location changes (city, country, hospital, rehab, home(s), school, workplace)

Use the Wheel of Emotions to color code each event on your timeline.

There is no right or wrong way to make your timeline.

Angry	Disgusted	Sad
Happy	Surprised	Bad
	Fearful	

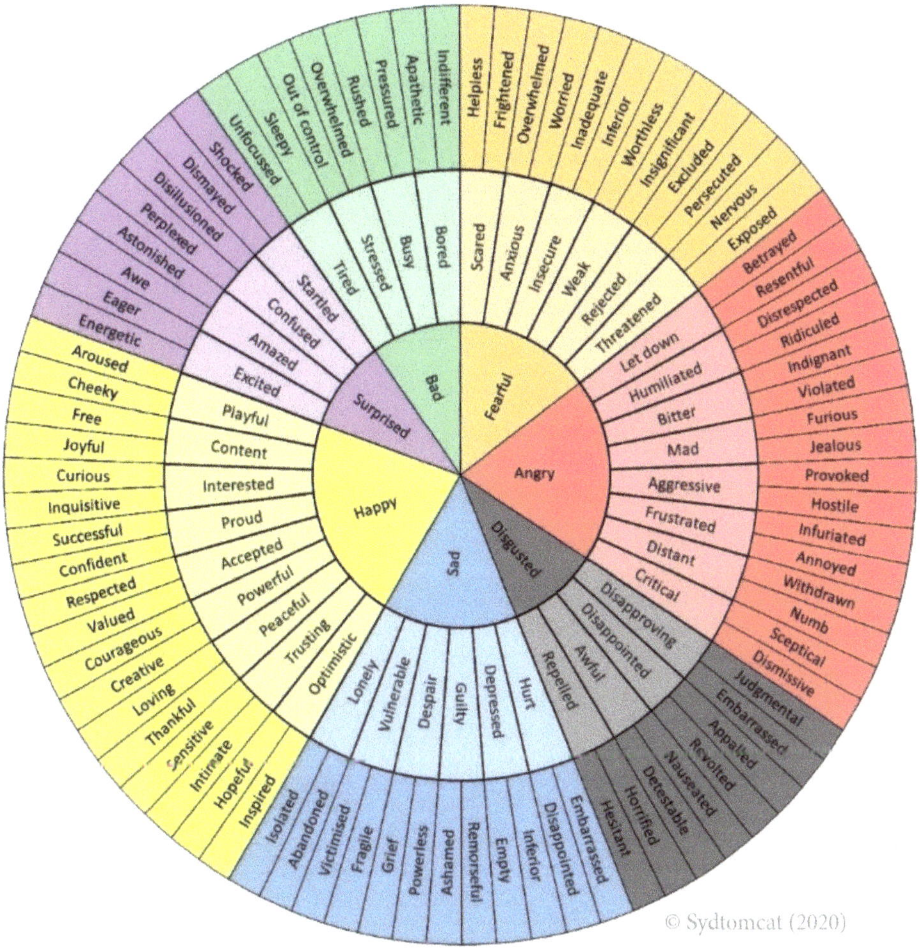

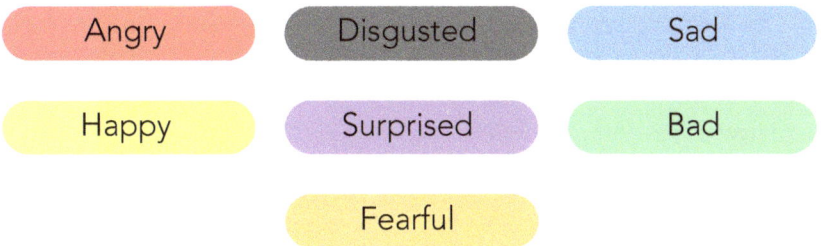

Personal Reflection Questions

- When did you feel close or far from your family, friends, community, coworkers, or God?

- How did they support you?

- How did family and friends care for you?

- Do you feel abandoned? By whom?

- Have I pushed people away (knowingly or unknowingly)?

Group Discussion for the Timeline

- What emotion(s) are most prevalent on your timeline?

- Who was present on your journey? Did you feel close or far from them?

- What needs (physical, emotional, mental, financial, spiritual) have been met? What needs do you wish had been met?

- Is an event on your timeline worth celebrating? How can you celebrate this event?

- Are you grateful for a person or event on the timeline?

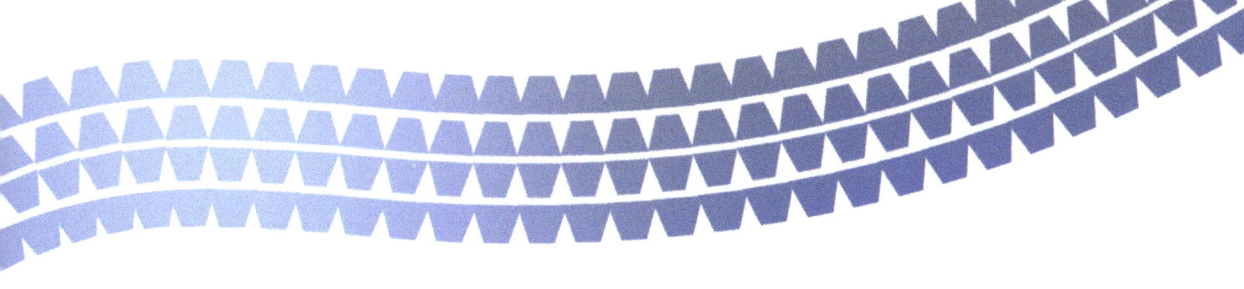

Naming What We've Lost

In life, loss is inevitable. Everyone knows this, yet in the core of most people it remains deeply denied— "This should not happen to me." It is for this reason that loss is the most difficult challenge one has to face as a human being.

— Dayananda Saraswati —

A major part of our journey after an unexpected disability or chronic condition is the loss that accompanies our situation. Oftentimes, we don't have the opportunity to name and grieve our losses. Until we can name our losses, we can't fully grieve, and we cannot make a healthy transition to the next step in our future.

Tangible and Intangible Losses

We can experience both tangible and intangible losses. Sometimes these are called primary and secondary losses. Tangible losses include physical (health), relational (family, friends, partners), or material (home or car). Intangible losses are more difficult to name and often create a greater sense of loss than tangible losses. But all losses are significant and deserve to be mourned.

Examples of Tangible Losses

- Death of a loved one
- Loss of function/health after the onset of physical disability
- Loss of a job or career

Examples of Intangible Losses

- Loss of identity
- Loss of income
- Loss of relationships or change in relationships (e.g., people treating you differently)
- Loss of confidence or self-image
- Loss of faith
- Loss of privacy
- Loss of independence
- Loss of holiday traditions
- Loss of dreams for the future
- Loss of safety and security
- Loss of being needed (or loss of your perception of being needed)

For example, a tangible loss from a spinal cord injury may be the inability to walk and the need to use a wheelchair or mobility aid. And an intangible loss that accompanies this may be the lack of community interaction due to inaccessible housing and transportation.

It's important to note that even when one loss appears similar to another, the impact is different. Two people may have the same disability but very different experiences.

Personal Reflection Time

- Take twenty to thirty minutes to list your tangible and intangible losses below.

- What do you believe about yourself based on the losses you listed? (Examples: I'm not valuable. I can overcome adversity.)

- What do you believe about others based on the losses you listed? (Examples: I cannot trust others to be there for me. My friends are supportive.)

Group Discussion Questions

- If you're willing, share a few of your greatest losses.

- What makes these losses significant in your life?

- What emotions do these losses produce when you think about them?

- Despite what we've lost, we can still use our abilities in new ways. What skills, gifts, or knowledge can you adapt to use in a different capacity?

Journey of Grief

*I sat with my anger long enough until she told me
her real name was grief.*

—C.S. Lewis—

Grief is our response to loss, and grieving is difficult. While it allows us to heal, grieving can be physically, emotionally, and spiritually exhausting. When we skip the grieving, it's tough to continue our journey in a healthy manner.

The Trauma Healing Institute developed a model of grief that is explained in the book *Healing the Wounds of Trauma* (2021). In The Grief Journey, we see three neighborhoods: the Neighborhood of Anger and Denial, the Neighborhood of No Hope, and the Neighborhood of New Beginnings.

The Grief Journey

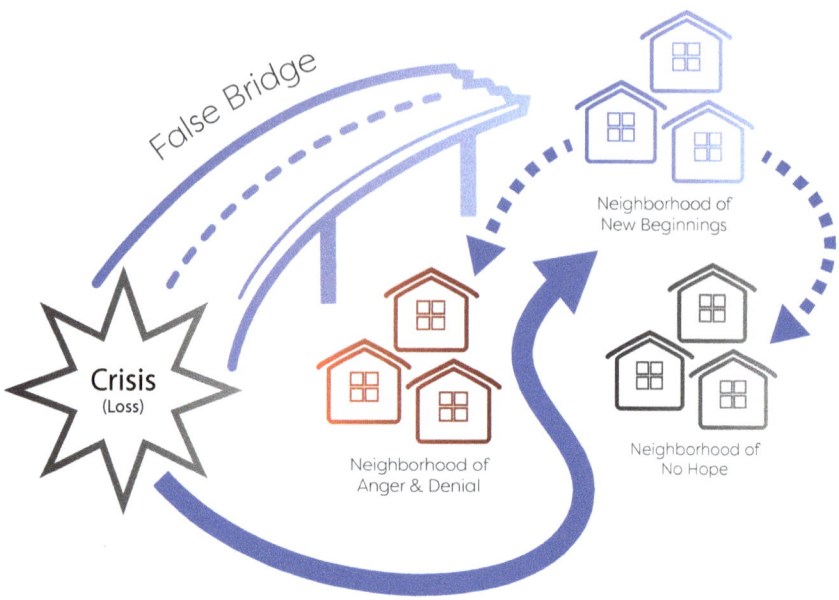

Adapted from *Healing the Wounds of Trauma*.
© 2021 ABS and SIL International. Used by Permission.

The Neighborhood of Anger and Denial

Anger and denial are natural reactions when we suffer loss. In this neighborhood, the numbness of denial may allow us to physically and emotionally cope with our surroundings until we are safe. We may blame others—or God—for our circumstances. Anger concerning our circumstances may come out in unexpected ways like lashing out at family, caregivers, or friends who are closest to us.

The Neighborhood of No Hope

The Neighborhood of No Hope is the darkest, loneliest, and scariest part of our journey. The future looks bleak. Our dreams for the future are gone. Depression may linger. The desire for our old life may feel overwhelming.

Yet we may have hope while feeling hope-less. Confused?

Merriam-Webster's Dictionary defines hope as "someone or something on which hopes are centered" (2023). This type of hope sustains us through the most challenging situations. Think of this as Hope, with a capital *H*. We also have hope for things in our future or the way we wish things would or could be. This hope, with a little *h*, can disappoint.

> **Hope** is faith in someone or something that is foundational to our purpose. Hope with a capital *H* is not determined by our present circumstances (e.g., if we are happy, have all we want, or have good physical health). Hope can be rooted in faith, religious or spiritual practice, or personal beliefs.

> **hope** is a desired outcome. Examples: the belief that research will provide a cure; the desire to have children; the expectation we will get married; the confidence that if we [work harder, pray more, eat right] we will [get better, have all we want, live an easier life].

Even if we have Hope, we can experience emotions in the Neighborhood of No Hope. Let's go back to the Wheel of Emotions from the Timeline. Some of these words may describe our experience in the Neighborhood of No Hope.

- abandoned
- apathetic
- ashamed
- confused
- depressed
- despair
- disappointed
- disillusioned
- dismayed
- empty
- excluded
- helpless
- indifferent
- inferior
- isolated
- lonely
- out of control
- overwhelmed
- powerless
- rejected
- scared
- stressed
- vulnerable (physically)
- worthless

The Neighborhood of No Hope is more than feeling depressed or suicidal.

The Neighborhood of New Beginnings

We enter the Neighborhood of New Beginnings once we grieve our losses. We begin to see possibilities for our future. We allow ourselves to experience life again. We are a different person in the Neighborhood of New Beginnings than we were at the beginning of our journey. But our journey required traversing through the Neighborhoods of Anger and Denial and No Hope before we entered New Beginnings.

The False Bridge

What if we never learned how to express anger or sadness? Or maybe expressing negative emotions wasn't allowed or modeled in our family growing up. Perhaps we want to "stay strong" and "keep a positive attitude" so we don't let family or friends down. We keep a smile on our faces and press forward. A person with a faith-based background may think a "true believer" doesn't get angry or depressed and avoids these feelings out of a false belief or guilt.

When we avoid these difficult feelings, we take the False Bridge.

Sometimes the False Bridge seems to be the best—or easiest—path to New Beginnings. While ignoring or stuffing our feelings may seem like a shortcut to the Neighborhood of New Beginnings, it only delays the journey to *truly* living in New Beginnings. When we blunt our sadness, anger, frustration, or hopelessness, we also blunt our ability to experience joy, acceptance, excitement, or love to their full extent. Numbing "negative" feelings also numbs "positive" feelings.

While the False Bridge isn't the ideal path, it may be all a person is capable of handling at the beginning of their journey.

We All Grieve Differently

The journey of grief will look different for each of us.

We all grieve differently and "visit" the neighborhoods at different times and in different orders. The important thing to remember is to not overstay our welcome in Anger, Denial, or No Hope. We may leave for a while and then return for a bit at a later time—even decades later. We just don't want to take up permanent residency in the Neighborhoods of Anger and Denial or No Hope.

One thing to mention is that with progressive diseases like muscular dystrophy, Parkinson's, or the aging process, we might cycle through The Grief Journey each time we experience additional loss.

Personal Reflection Questions

- What were the rules for expressing emotion growing up? In your family, who showed you positive or negative examples of expressing emotion?

- What have family, friends, or strangers said or done that makes you feel alone in your grief?

- What have family, friends, or strangers said or done that makes you feel comforted in your grief?

- Have you lost the ability to do an activity that allows you to express emotions? Examples: going for a run, writing, art, sports, or playing an instrument.

- Have you tried to "stuff down" your emotions?

- Have you used activities or substances to dull or escape from your emotions? If so, when? How often?

    ____ Food (overeating or restricting)

    ____ Prescription or illegal drugs

    ____ Alcohol

    ____ Pornography

    ____ Pursuing lifelong research, therapy, or "cures" or going into debt in that pursuit

    ____ Binge-watching television

    ____ Reading/audiobooks/podcasts

    ____ Social media

    ____ Working too much

    ____ Sleeping

    ____ Shopping

- Have you taken out your emotions on people around you? Who?

- Do you have Hope?

- Do you have specific hopes for the future?

Group Discussion Questions

- What neighborhoods have you visited?

- Have you ever felt tempted—or pressured—to take the False Bridge?

- If you feel comfortable sharing, what unhealthy activities do you use to dull your emotions?

Activity: Lament
(Optional)

Oftentimes, it's difficult to find an "acceptable" way to express our feelings of sadness, anger, and depression. One way to acknowledge these overwhelming feelings is through writing a lament.

Lament is the practice of expressing grief. We can read examples of lament in ancient civilizations including Sumer, Greece, China, and the Near East. Over one third of psalms in the Hebrew Bible are psalms of lament.

A lament in the book of Psalms has at least six parts:

- A call to God
- A complaint
- A cry for help or a request
- Sometimes an admission of innocence or guilt
- Remembrance of God's faithfulness in the past
- A promise to trust in God

Read the examples below. Identify the parts of the lament.

Psalm 13 (New Living Translation)

[1] O Lord, how long will you forget me? Forever?

How long will you look the other way?

[2] How long must I struggle with anguish in my soul,

with sorrow in my heart every day?

How long will my enemy have the upper hand?

[3] Turn and answer me, O Lord my God!

Restore the sparkle to my eyes, or I will die.

[4] Don't let my enemies gloat, saying, "We have defeated him!"

Don't let them rejoice at my downfall.

[5] But I trust in your unfailing love.

I will rejoice because you have rescued me.

[6] I will sing to the Lord

because he is good to me.

A Lament by Jenny

Oh, God, listen to me!

    What have I done to deserve this life?

I despise feeling like a burden. I suffocate from the weight

    of the financial cost of disability. I fear dying alone.

Please keep my butt healed (just keeping this real).

    Make my pain bearable,

    and give me what I need—and maybe even what I want.

I've trusted you. I still do, but

    sometimes

        in the darkness

            the future overwhelms me.

When life gets hard, help me remember how

    you've provided in the past.

I can't do this on my own, so I need to trust in you.

I'll say it again and try to believe it.

    My trust is in you.

Personal Exercise

Spend some time alone and write a lament. While a lament doesn't need to have all six parts, it must include a complaint. Express your anger, fear, frustration, anguish, sadness, and/or despair to God. Feel free to be creative in your lament: scribble out a prayer, write a song or a poem, or sketch a piece of art.

Group Discussion

- What was the hardest or easiest part of writing a lament?

- Identify one or two emotions you felt (positive or negative) while crafting your lament.

- What are some other thoughts you have about this exercise? Will you do it again?

- Do you practice lamenting in other ways? (Journaling, listening to music, praying, etc.)

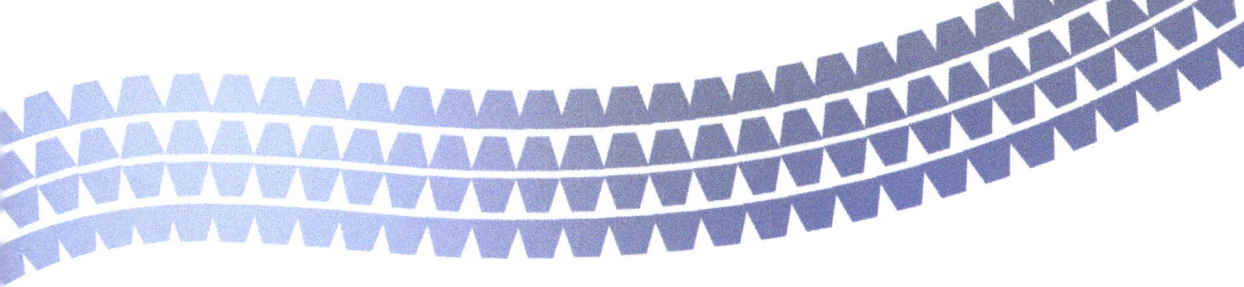

Change and Transition

Change is inevitable. Growth is optional.
—John C. Maxwell—

With a disability or chronic medical condition, life changes. How we go through our everyday activities may change. Simply getting out of bed can be an ordeal.

The question is: are you willing to transition to life with a disability?

Change and transition seem like they mean the same. But there's a big difference. Change happens to us—we are not in control. It is a sign that one thing has ended and something new is beginning. Transition is the psychological and emotional process inside of us as we respond to and adapt to change. It's internal. Emotional. Mental. We choose how—or if—we adjust our lives to the new path we are on.

Look at the Transition Bridge on the next page. Examine the stages of transition we experience after a disability.

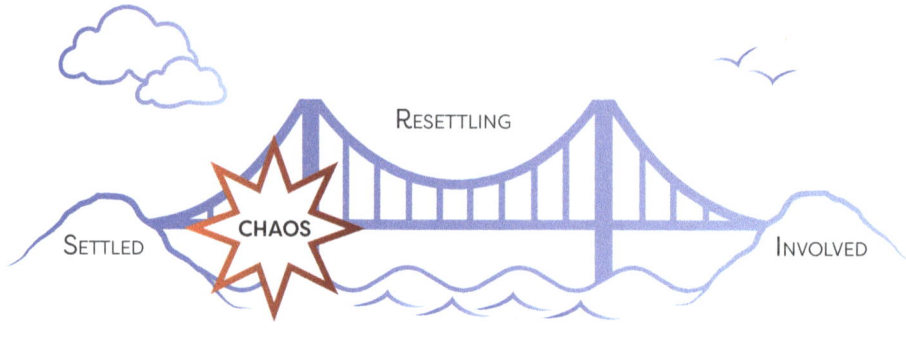

The Transition Bridge
Adapted from David. C. Pollock

Settled

Before our disability, we were settled. We knew who we were in relation to others, and we knew how to navigate the world. We understood our role in our family, workplace, and among our peers.

Chaos

Upon our disability or symptoms of a chronic health condition, we may feel completely out of control. We may have no control over when we get up, go to the bathroom, or go to sleep. We may feel that no one understands our situation. And, in reality, no one does. We might feel that our family or friends or medical professionals should be at our beck and call, or we may lash out when they can't meet our physical or emotional needs as we would like. We might see friends or family leave because they can't deal with the situation. We may even push away family and friends. As we see others living a "normal" life, we might resent that we don't know what our future holds.

Resettling

As we try to set out on a journey on this new path, we may feel like spectators of our own life. We're on the sidelines watching people work or play where we once flourished. Relationships take effort and transparency. We may misinterpret others' behaviors or misread them and their intentions. Slowly, we may listen to or ask questions of a person or peer mentor who has "been there, done that." We start to see a bit of hope and hesitantly begin to play with the cards we've been dealt.

Involved

During these transition phases, we grieve. Depression, hopelessness, anger, and denial make our journey bumpy and difficult to navigate. But if we allow the internal emotional transition to occur, we get involved again. The people in our lives—possibly old ones, maybe new—encourage and accept us. More importantly, we accept ourselves. We get to know others with similar experiences. We feel like we belong again. It may not be the way we belonged before, but we still feel a sense of belonging. We may have less energy or time, but we learn to adapt to our abilities—even when we don't like the changes.

Transition can be scary. For transition to be accomplished, we must be willing to adapt to the new world in which we live.

The Experience of Transition to Disability

In each stage of the Transition Bridge, we experience changes in how we view ourselves in the world, how we interact with the world around us, and the emotions we experience as a result of our disabilities.

Study the model of the Experience of Transition to Disability below. What statements can you relate to?

The Experience of Transition to Disability
Adapted from David. C. Pollock

	SETTLED	**CHAOS**	**RESETTLING**	**INVOLVED**
My Status	Belonging	Statusless	New Beginning	Belonging
	• Part of an "in" group • Have a role • Have a status • I'm known and know others	• They don't understand • I have no control • Different • I have knowledge I can't use	• Superficial • Uncertain of my position with family, friends, and society • On the sidelines	• I'm known • I know others • Rebuilding position, role, and status • Engaged with family, friends
Social Experience	Committed	Disengaged	Re-engaging	Committed
	• Responsible • Responsive to physical and emotional needs	• Self-centered • Unknown future • Relationships in flux (some supportive and responsive, some not)	• Observer • Must initiate relationships • Searching for/accepting of peer mentor(s)	• Belonging • Involved • Comforting behavior • Concern for others
Emotional Experience	Intimacy	Denial/Anxiety	Vulnerability	Intimacy
	• Confident • Secure	• Resentful • Depressed, angry • Ashamed • Loss of self-esteem • Loss of normalcy	• Transparent • Scared • Ambivalent • Hopeful • Easily frustrated • Determined • Looking forward	• Rebuilding self-confidence • Rebuilding security • Feel accepted

Personal Reflection Questions

- What stage(s) are you in right now?

- What are you thinking? Feeling? Wanting?

- How has the way you view yourself changed since your disability or chronic condition?

- How has the way you view others changed since your disability or chronic condition?

- How have your relationships changed with your family, friends, and community?

- View life from the perspective of your parent, sibling, spouse, significant other, and friend. What stage are they in? How has their life been impacted?

- Are you willing to initiate relationships? If not, what feels scary?

- What one thing will you commit to do?

Group Discussion Questions

- Where do you experience a sense of belonging?

- How have you intentionally built new relationships?

- How are you rebuilding self-confidence?

- What is the best advice a peer has shared with you about living with a disability?

- If you are willing to share, what have you committed to do?

Paradox

*I have suffered many losses, but I still have
a deep capacity for joy and pleasure.*

—Alice Wong—

In the midst of pain, suffering, and grief, we may see little light at the end of the tunnel. In fact, we may believe we can never be happy, confident, or fulfilled again.

Is it possible to experience pain and loss and joy and adventure at the same time?

Yes, it is.

We can learn to live in a state of paradox.

What is Paradox?

Paradox is a situation that is seemingly contradictory.

The first line of *A Tale of Two Cities* by Charles Dickens states, "It was the best of times, it was the worst of times."

These are two *opposite* yet *equally true* statements. The same can be true in our lives with disability.

Below are two examples of paradox:

- I feel alone *and* My friends are supportive.
- Life is crappy (sometimes literally) *and* I enjoy the opportunities I have.

The above statements are equally true and valid. One doesn't negate the validity of the other.

Sandy Wright-Smith (1997) uses a pair of ducks to describe the concept of paradox.

A "Yay Duck" is the positive statement of paradox. It was the best of times. My friends are supportive. The "Yuck Duck" is the negative experience of a paradoxical situation. It was the worst of times. I feel alone.

The Yuck Ducks may win out on some days, but with practice, we can look for the Yay Ducks—even if it seems insignificant. The Yuck Ducks and Yay Ducks are equally valid and true.

Now and Not Yet

The diagram below is another way of looking at paradox.

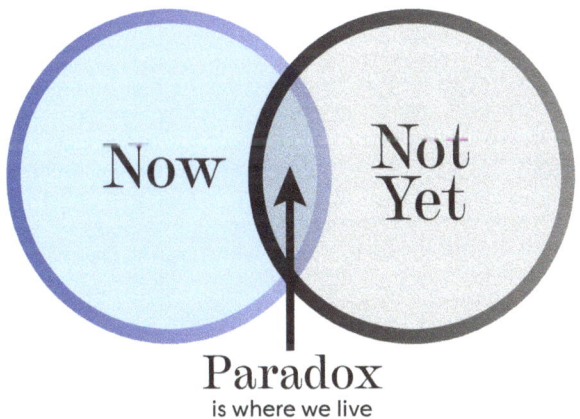

On the one hand, we live in the Now; on the other hand, we look forward to the Not Yet. Where these two circles overlap is our paradox. We wait, or work, or hope for the Not Yet. But more importantly, we *live*. Not just exist. Not just take up space. We give ourselves permission to live abundantly in the Now until our Not Yet comes to fruition. We live in the tension of paradox.

Defining Acceptance

When we talk about acceptance, especially as someone nears the Neighborhood of New Beginnings, it's important to ask how one defines "accept."

If a person thinks that accepting their disability means giving up on life, then they might be reluctant to "accept" it. They are right not to give up! Acceptance is better described as giving yourself permission to transition and adapt to life with a disability. Acceptance is a process and can take years. And that's okay.

We can think of acceptance as the *willingness* to live in the tension of paradox.

Personal Reflection Questions:

- Name three Yay Ducks and three Yuck Ducks from the past week.

- How would you describe your Now?

- How would you describe your Not Yet?

- Have you given yourself permission to adapt and transition to life with a disability?

- Are you hesitant to "accept" your disability because you feel you're giving up hope on a good or full life?

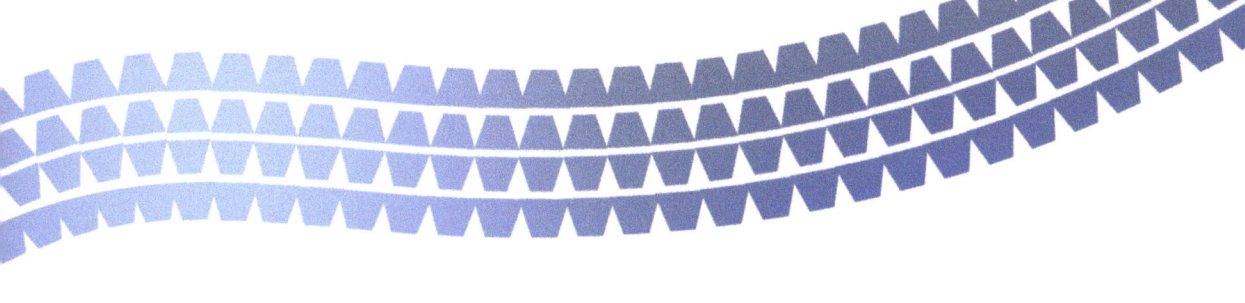

Stress, Trauma, and Coping Strategies

Stress can be managed, relieved and lessened, but never eliminated.
—Gudjon Bergmann—

Life with a disability can be stressful. It is often a full-time job in addition to our already full lives. How can we maintain our emotional and spiritual health with the additional stress that accompanies a disability?

What Is Stress?

Stress involves environmental events or factors (stressors), our reactions to the stress, and the resources we use to cope with the stress (Koteskey and Seitz 2023).

Picture the resources we have to cope with stress as a bank account. Let's say we have $1,000 saved up for emergencies. When unexpected events occur, we tap into the account. A tire on our vehicle needs to be replaced. Thankfully, we've got that covered. A kitchen appliance breaks. We may not like it, but we can tap into savings. Then health insurance denies a claim, and our account is suddenly in the negative. When stressful situations from life with a disability bombard us, we may no longer have sufficient resources to "pay for" the stress of life.

Where Does Stress Come from?

Let's first get something straight: not all stress is bad. Stress can make us work hard, set and accomplish goals, and meet deadlines. Some people even *like* stress. Positive events such as a marriage, the birth of a child, a new job, or retirement can be stressful. These events still require us to transition and draw on our resources.

The constant onslaught of stressors without sufficient resources impacts our long-term emotional, physical, mental, and spiritual health.

Stress comes from:

- Life events (health changes, marriage, employment status, children)
- Daily hassles (transportation, household chores, personal care)
- Situational factors that we have little control over (sickness, chronic pain, caregivers, bladder and bowel issues)

- Traumatic events (medical procedures, lack of safety or security, car accidents, falls)
- Comparison (expectations we have of ourselves or that we perceive from others)

Normal Reactions to Stress

It's normal to experience physical, emotional, behavioral, cognitive, and spiritual reactions to stress.

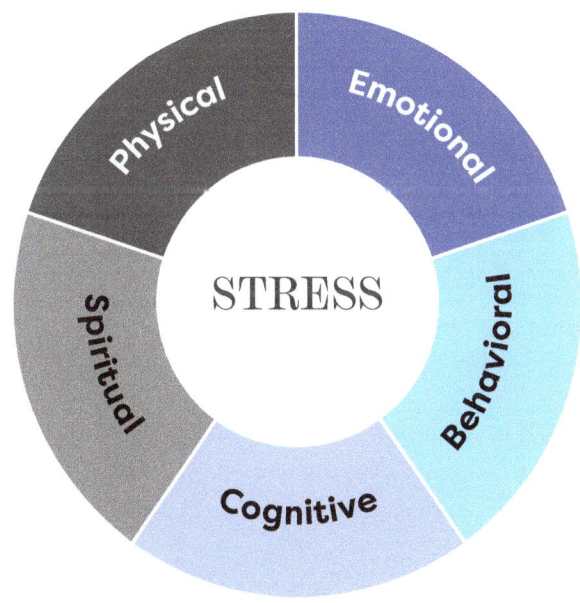

Personal Reflection Questions

Circle the stress reactions you have experienced (and that you do not experience without stress).

Physical (our body's response):

Headache   Tight neck/shoulders   Stomachache

Diarrhea   Fatigue/exhaustion   Insomnia   Heart disease

Decreased immune system   Weight gain or loss

Emotional (how we feel):

Anxiety   Difficulty concentrating   Depression   Anger

Frustration   Denial   Fear   Feeling abandoned or isolated

Behavioral (how we act):

Changes in communication   Withdrawal   Emotional outbursts

Overeating/undereating   Hyper-alertness

Using medicine/drugs or alcohol inappropriately

Changes in activity level

Cognitive (how we think):

Lack of concentration   Memory disturbances
Difficulty with decisions   Confusion   Worry   Self-blame
Blaming others

Spiritual (our belief system):

Questioning why   Blaming God   Feeling a lack of purpose
Feeling abandoned by God   Difficulty praying
Preoccupation with spiritual meaning

All of these are normal reactions to stress.

Personal or Group Activity

Groups: Use six large sticky poster boards, a dry-erase board, or—if meeting online—share your screen and record participants' answers.

Using the acronym STRESS, name the stressors you experience in each category.

S Social

T Temperament

R Resource

E Enviromental

S Situational

S Spiritual

- **Social** stress is the tension we feel when interacting with others.

- **Temperament** stress is created by our own temperament and personality (introvert, extrovert, organized, creative).

- **Resource** stress is created by a lack of sufficient resources to accomplish our goals or a lack of control over those resources. While money is a resource, resources also include time and energy.

- **Environmental** stress is created by our response to the environment around us.

- **Situational** stress comes from an inability to be certain about some aspects of our lives.

- **Spiritual** stress occurs when our relationship with God, others, nature, music, or creativity is hindered.

What Is Trauma?

Trauma occurs when a person experiences intense fear, helplessness, or horror. Many of us have experienced trauma from the circumstances that caused our disabilities or because of the medical procedures we have undergone.

We felt an overwhelming sense of helplessness when utterly dependent on another human for the bare necessities of life. We remember with horror the physical pain we experienced that no drug could relieve.

It's important to note that a procedure doesn't need to go "wrong" to be traumatic.

We also experience day-to-day traumas that add up over time. We have another infection with all the side effects that accompany antibiotics. A caregiver doesn't show up—again. Each night, we get into bed to check for a pressure sore with the memory of an extended period in bed—and fear haunts us that this will happen again. When we require medical tests, we experience additional unsuccessful blood draws or IV sticks.

Symptoms of Trauma

The symptoms of trauma are very similar to stress symptoms. However, responses to trauma may be more severe and include inability to sleep, panic attacks, debilitating anxiety, nightmares, substance abuse, numbing all emotion, depression, or—in some cases—post-traumatic stress disorder (PTSD). Trauma can also impact our hopes and expectations for the future and cause us to believe we won't experience the typical milestones of life in education, relationships, or work and volunteer opportunities (Center for Substance Abuse Treatment 2014).

When a situation inexplicably brings tears, fear, or panic, our bodies may be responding to trauma. Trauma is not "just" an emotional or psychological response. Our body reacts to trauma at a visceral level. Our brain and autonomic and sympathetic nervous systems tell our body we aren't safe. Chemicals get released into our bloodstream, and parts of our brain shut down, putting us into survival mode.

Additional Trauma Resources

Trauma will not "go away" until it is fully processed. While the questions and activities in this workbook allow us to reflect upon the traumatic events we've experienced, some of us may need a trained trauma therapist. Please see the resources at the end of the workbook to find additional trauma-related help.

Personal Reflection Questions

- Have you experienced an event where you felt intense fear, helplessness, or horror?

- How has this event (or events) impacted you emotionally, socially, physically, and spiritually?

- Do you need to get help from a professional to begin processing the trauma you've experienced?

- What is the first step you need to do to get help? By what date will you do this?

Coping Strategies for Stress and Trauma

Let's discuss a few positive coping strategies when we experience stress or our body's reaction to trauma. These exercises help balance the emotional and rational sides of our brains. When we are stressed or anxious, the emotional part of our brain often overtakes the rational.

Exercise One: Deep Breathing

Slowly inhale through your nose, hold your breath, then exhale through your mouth. Repeat four times.

> ***Inhale*** – one, two, three, four
>
> ***Hold*** – one, two, three, four
>
> ***Exhale*** – one, two, three, four

If you can't inhale, exhale, or hold your breath to the count of four, begin by counting to two.

Exercise Two: Rhythmic Tapping

Tap in a rhythmic pattern, right-left, right-left. This exercise can be adapted according to your physical ability.

Use your hands to rhythmically tap one of these areas: the collarbone, the corners of your eyes, or each knee. Slowly alternate right and left hands for one minute.

To adapt this exercise:

- Move your eyes from right to left
- Blink your right eye, then your left eye
- Shrug your right shoulder, then the left
- Lift your right heel off the ground, then the left
- Extend your right wrist, then your left

If you are unable to tap, this exercise is just as effective if someone taps for you.

Exercise Three: Listen to Your Heartbeat

If your mind is racing, focus on listening to and feeling your heartbeat. This is most useful at night when it's quiet.

Exercise Four: Break It Down

When you feel overwhelmed and don't think you can make it through an entire day, break the day into segments. For example, morning to lunch, lunch to dinner, and dinner to bedtime. If that still feels too long, break the day into one-hour or half-hour segments. Even fifteen minutes, if necessary.

When you successfully get through the time segment, reinforce your accomplishment and congratulate yourself that you did it—and can do it again.

Exercise Five: Imagine a Container

When you have multiple concerns running through your head, imagine a container in which you can place your thoughts, worries, and fears.

Describe in detail your container. It must have a lid.

- What material is it made of?
- What color is it?
- What size is the container?
- How does the lid lock in place?
- What do you want to call your container?

Picture yourself placing your concerns into the container, closing the lid, and leaving the container behind. How does this feel?

Instead of stuffing your emotions, you are setting them aside for a time.

When you have the ability and time, "pull out" one item from your container and allow yourself to process it. Talk to a friend or counselor, journal about the item, and/or pray about it.

Refill Your Cup

We cannot give what we do not possess.
We cannot help but give what we do possess.

—Peter Scazzero—

We often hear proverbs or sayings about the importance of "filling your cup." With all the stressors we experience with disability, how and where can our emotional, mental, physical, and spiritual cups be refilled?

What are some characteristics of these cups?

-
-
-
-
-
-

Cups are common. They come in different sizes, shapes, and colors. Cups serve different purposes. Some are fragile while others are sturdy. Cups can be emptied and refilled. If not cared for properly, cups break and can no longer be used unless they are repaired.

Our emotional, physical, and spiritual resources, like cups, need to be refilled. Rest is one way to refill our cups. In *Tender Care*, authors Reagon Wilson and David Kronbach explain that rest "goes beyond the physical and is often used in context with the spiritual and social aspect of our beings" (Wilson and Kronbach, 2010, 97).

Characteristics of Rest and Refilling

Rest and refilling our cups will look different for everyone. For some people, it means spending time alone; others prefer a meal with close friends. Some refill their resources with a workout, while other people prefer to sit outside with a good book.

But rest and refilling must be intentional. It cannot—or will not—happen on its own.

Personal Reflection Questions

- Do you need rest for the deepest parts of your body, mind, and spirit?

- What refreshes and restores your body, mind, and spirit? Name some activities, interests, and hobbies.

- Do you typically refill your resources alone or in community?

- If you've lost your previous sources of rest and refilling (e.g., physical activity, walking in nature, taking a long drive, having a hot shower), name activities you can adapt to refill your emotional, physical, and spiritual resources.

Finding Meaning and Purpose

He who has a "why" to live for can bear almost any "how."
—Friedrich Nietzsche—

To thrive in this world of Disability, we need to find purpose and meaning in life. We might feel this is impossible when so much has been stripped away from us while we are also managing the loss, grief, and daily stressors.

Yet Viktor Frankl (1992), a psychiatrist, neurologist, and concentration camp survivor, states that we must find significance in our lives to survive and thrive. Frankl believes our meaning in life comes from three primary sources: pursuing life tasks, loving selflessly, and finding courage and meaning in suffering. Lozeron (2019) summarizes these three sources of meaning on the next page.

Setting Goals and Pursuing New Experiences

To find purpose, we need to set goals and be open to new experiences (even when it's scary or uncomfortable). We must continue to learn. We need to believe we have unique talents, skills, and abilities that can make an impact—even if it's just on one person. When we pursue goals and new experiences, we find meaning in life.

Loving Selflessly

When loving selflessly, we want to help others succeed and achieve their full potential. We can be a mentor. We may reframe our need for assistance as an opportunity for others to serve and learn new skills. We listen to and talk with those who are lonely or hurting. When we desire to help others, our life has a purpose.

Finding Meaning in Suffering

As we look at our circumstances, how do we choose to respond? Remember we decide how to adjust and transition to our new path. Do we react in anger? With humor? Determination? Do we learn to have empathy for others? The person whom we choose to become gives meaning to our suffering.

We can find our meaning and purpose by discovering our goals, who we can help, and who we are becoming. During our most challenging circumstances, we must cling to our meaning and purpose. This knowledge needs to be deeply embedded in our souls. We have to believe our lives can "create a ripple effect that spills over into the lives of people [we] may never meet" (Smith 2021, 216). To do this, we must discover our purpose and meaning.

Personal Reflection Questions

Take some time to answer the following questions. Think about activities throughout your lifespan. What similarities exist between your hobbies, career(s), or projects? Don't exclude an answer because you believe your disability or physical condition may limit you.

- What do you love to do?

- What are your talents, strengths, and unique abilities?

- What causes are you passionate about?

- What goals or new experiences do you want to plan for your future? (Don't be afraid to think big!)

- Who is in your life right now? How can you help them achieve their full potential? How can you selflessly love them?

- How have you grown through your experience with disability? Do you like who you are becoming?

- How do you want people to remember you when you are at the end of your life?

Your purpose and meaning statement:

I will use my _____ **to** _____ **so**
(talents, strengths, abilities)   *(what I love to do)*

_____.
(what I am passionate about)

Conclusion

I hope working through these lessons has been a journey worth the effort. In my own life, the tools I've included in this book have been both valuable and necessary.

After my injury at age sixteen, I took the False Bridge. This wasn't an intentional divergence. I simply didn't know how else to navigate the complicated and unfamiliar world of Disability. Ignoring my feelings was easier—and familiar.

Over time, I met people with whom I could relate. I could talk with them without shame about bladder and bowel issues and the need for personal care. We could discuss the frustrations of skin breakdown, the changes in body image, and the financial burdens of a disability. They "got it" in a way my closest friends and family could not. Forging those relationships was the first step on my journey into the Neighborhood of New Beginnings.

But I don't want to make my journey sound like it has been a nonstop flight to my final destination.

Several years ago, I'd had an especially difficult day. I was drained physically, emotionally, and mentally. I turned on a podcast to help me unwind as I got ready for bed, but even that felt too taxing on my brain. I decided to decompress by listening to classical music instead.

My body and mind relaxed as *Moonlight Sonata* hummed through the speakers. I had played this piece of music on the piano before my injury. Each note of the song was familiar—hauntingly familiar. Even thirty years after my injury, I could feel each finger touch the keys of an invisible piano.

What happened next took me by surprise.

My eyes welled up with tears. The loss of playing piano rushed over me in a wave of unexpected grief. I didn't try to stuff the feelings or tell myself this wasn't worth mourning since I hadn't played piano for three decades. I named and acknowledged my loss and grieved it. Then I continued on my journey the next day.

If you are stuck feeling anger, denial, or depression, please don't hesitate to reach out for support. Peer mentoring programs, support groups, and adaptive sports and recreation programs are places where you can meet people who can relate to life with a disability. A counselor or therapist can help you work through this book and recover from trauma you may have experienced from your disability or subsequent medical interventions.

In my book *Live the Impossible*, I summarize my journey with a spinal cord injury:

> The path set before me at age sixteen was full of potholes, cobblestones, and gravel. It continues to be bumpy, uncom-

fortable, and tiresome. But it's also been beautiful, rewarding, and adventurous (Smith 2021, 3).

Life is a paradox. I hope that despite the potholes you encounter on your journey, you, too, will experience beautiful, rewarding, and unexpected adventures. This is not the life I would have chosen. But the journey has forced me to grow emotionally, mentally, and spiritually in ways I wouldn't have otherwise.

If you've gone through this material with a group of fellow sojourners, my hope is you've learned from each other. Always remember that you do not have to travel alone.

Let's continue to support one another as we take this journey. Together, we can thrive—not just survive—in this foreign land called Disability.

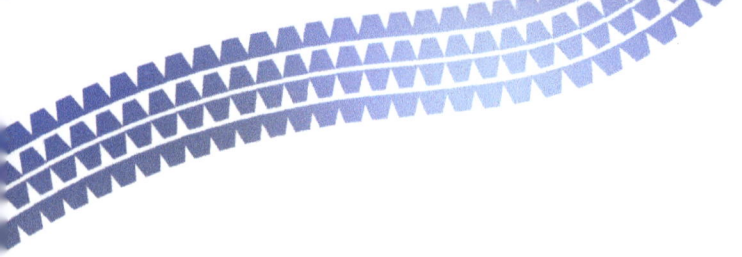

Additional Resources

Trauma Resources

Trauma Healing Institute: https://traumahealinginstitute.org/
Trauma therapists in the US:
    https://www.psychologytoday.com/us/therapists/trauma-and-ptsd
Trauma Survivors Network:
    https://www.traumasurvivorsnetwork.org/

Peer Support and Support Groups

ALS Association: https://www.als.org/local-support
American Cancer Society's Cancer Survivors Network:
    https://csn.cancer.org/
American Stroke Association: https://www.stroke.org/
Amputee Coalition:
    https://www.amputee-coalition.org/
Backbones (spinal cord injury/disease):
    https://backbonesonline.com/
Brian Injury Association of America:
    https://www.biausa.org/find-bia
Crohn's & Colitis Foundation:
    https://www.crohnscolitisfoundation.org/community-support
More Than Walking (spinal cord injury/disease):
    https://www.morethanwalking.com/
Muscular Dystrophy Association: https://www.mda.org/

National Multiple Sclerosis Society:
   https://www.nationalmssociety.org/Resources-Support
Parkinson's Foundation:
   https://www.parkinson.org/resources-support
United Spinal Association (spinal cord injury/disease):
   https://unitedspinal.org/peer-support-program/

Crisis Support

National Suicide and Crisis Lifeline: Dial 988 in the United States

Suggested Schedule for Groups

In a group setting, take at least eight weeks to go through this material. Two hours is sufficient time for each session. Even though the workbook is short, the reading and exercises take time and emotional energy. Prior to each session, participants should schedule time to read through the material and answer the Personal Reflection and Group Discussion Questions.

Week 1: Introduction
Group Introductions and Rules
Why Take Time to Reflect?
Homework: Timeline

Week 2: Timeline Review
(discuss insights, Personal Reflection and Group Discussion Questions)

Week 3: Naming What We've Lost

Week 4: Journey of Grief
Homework: Lament (Optional)

Week 5: Lament Sharing (one or two participants)
Change and Transition
Paradox

Week 6: Stress, Trauma, and Coping Strategies

Week 7: Refill Your Cup
Finding Meaning and Purpose

Week 8: Closing Session
- Wrap up the group by asking what was most helpful about their experience

- Allow group members to share their next steps

- Agree on how or if participants will continue to communicate

- Request any administrative needs (e.g., contact information, surveys)

Group Introduction and Rules

If you use this material in a group setting, allow group members to introduce themselves and discuss the group rules.

Group Introduction

- Name
- Location (if meeting virtually)
- Disability and date of onset
- Anything else you want the group to know

Groups Rules

If you choose to take this journey with a group, please adopt the following rules so everyone feels safe to share their story.

- Maintain confidentiality. What is discussed in the group stays in the group. Often, one of the greatest losses after a disability is privacy. Let's make this group a safe place.

- Decide on other confidentiality rules, if desired. For example, will you communicate or acknowledge each other outside of the group? On social media?

- Listen to others, avoid interrupting, and take turns speaking.

- Speak without judging others.

- Understand this is an educational support group. It is not therapy or counseling.

- Feel free to express your beliefs, but do not pressure others to hold to the same point of view.

- If a person shares that they would like to harm themselves or another person, or is experiencing abuse, the facilitator may need to contact the proper authorities.

References

Center for Substance Abuse Treatment. 2014. *Trauma-Informed Care in Behavioral Health Services*. Rockville, MD: Substance Abuse and Mental Health Administration. https://www.ncbi.nlm.nih.gov/books/NBK207191/

Ergenbright, Dana, Stacey Conard, and Mary Crickmore. 2021. *Healing the Wounds of Trauma: How the Church Can Help (Stories from North America), Facilitator Guide for Healing Groups 2021 Edition*. Philadelphia: American Bible Society.

Frankl, Viktor. 1992. *Man's Search for Meaning: An Introduction to Logotherapy*. Boston: Beacon Press.

Koteskey, Ron, and Marty Seitz. "Stewardship of Self for Christian Workers: Stress." Missionary Care. Accessed on October 13, 2023. https://missionarycare.com/stewardship-stress.html.

Lozeron, Nathan. "Man's Search for Meaning by Viktor Frankl." Video. *Productivity Game*, July 25, 2019. https://youtu.be/YYBg9_069g-g?si=gP52CbIvuBrWJ9k3.

Merriam-Webster Dictionary. "Hope." Accessed September 10, 2023. https://www.merriam-webster.com/dictionary/hope.

Smith, Jenny. 2021. *Live the Impossible: How a Wheelchair Has Taken Me Places I Never Dared to Imagine*. Louisville, KY: Significant Publications.

Smith, Jenny. 2024. "The Transition Bridge." Adapted from unpublished graphic by David C. Pollock.

Smith, Jenny. 2024. "The Transition Experience." Adapted from unpublished graphic by David C. Pollock.

Sydtomcat. "Emotions Wheel." Wikimedia Commons. August 2020. https://commons.wikimedia.org/wiki/File:Emotions_wheel.png

Wilson, Reagon, and David Kronbach. 2010. *Tender Care*. Elkhorn, WI: Barnabas Books.

Wright-Smith, Sandy. 1997. *Children's Intercultural Program*. Training material for SPLICE. Palmer Lake, CO: Mission Training International.

About the Author

Jenny Smith, M.Ed.

When Jenny was sixteen years old, she sustained a C6-7 spinal cord injury, leaving her paralyzed from the chest down. After completing her master's degree in counseling psychology, she distributed wheelchairs for eight years in developing countries. For over thirteen years, she supported cross-cultural workers as they served overseas.

By coming alongside people with spinal cord injuries and chronic medical conditions, Jenny hopes to support and encourage others in their emotional, physical, and spiritual health as they adapt to life with a disability. She provides education, practical solutions, resources, and hope so people can live full and productive lives on her website, JennySmithRollsOn.com.

Jenny stays physically active rowing on the Ohio River with Louisville Adaptive Rowing. Reading historical fiction and writing are other hobbies she enjoys.

In her book *Live the Impossible*, Jenny tells her story of living with a spinal cord injury and shares her message that we can all live the impossible even when life doesn't go as planned.

> Website: JennySmithRollsOn.com
> YouTube: youtube.com/JennySmithRollsOn
> Facebook: facebook.com/JennySmithRollsOn
> Instagram: instagram.com/jenny.smith.rolls.on
> LinkedIn: linkedin.com/in/jenny-smith-rolls-on

www.ingramcontent.com/pod-product-compliance
Lightning Source LLC
Chambersburg PA
CBHW042027100526
44587CB00029B/4327